So Lit-C Hemingway's Old Man and the Sea

By

The Editors

of Squid Ink Classics

Includes Over 100 MLA 8 Style Citations for Scholarly Secondary Sources, Peer-Reviewed Journal Articles and Critical Essays

Squid Ink Classics

So Lit-Crit Hemingway's Old Man and the Sea

By

The Editors

of Squid Ink Classics

Includes Over 100 MLA 8 Style Citations for Scholarly Secondary Sources, Peer-Reviewed Journal Articles and Critical Essays

Squid Ink Classics

So Lit-Crit Guides Text copyright 2017 by Squid Ink Classics

An Imprint of Laughing Gull Classics

All rights reserved.

Printed in the United States of America.

No part of this book may be used or reproduced

in any manner whatsoever without written

permission except in the case of true quotations

embodied in critical articles and reviews.

For information address: Squid Ink Classics online.

Library of Congress Cataloging in Publication Data

Squid Ink Classics

ISBN-13:
978-1978103948

ISBN-10:
1978103948

Published by Squid Ink Classics

Boston, Massachusetts

Contents

What are literary criticisms?

Who writes literary criticisms?

Where do I find literary criticisms?

When do I use literary criticisms?

Why do I need literary criticisms?

How do I find literary criticisms?

Over 100 MLA Style Citations for Scholarly Secondary Sources, Journal Articles, and Critical Essays

WHAT?

What are literary criticisms?

Literary criticisms are scholarly essays that critically analyze a piece of literature.

WHO?

Who writes literary criticisms?

Literary criticisms are written by scholars, most often college English professors, who spend years, sometimes their entire lifetime devoted to the study of one author or one author's work.

WHERE?

Where do I find literary criticisms?

Literary criticisms are published in peer-reviewed or scholarly journals and can be found in online literary databases available through your library.

WHEN?

When do I use literary criticisms?

You use literary criticisms when you are writing a research paper for your English classes as your secondary sources.

WHY?

Why do I need literary criticisms?

Because your teacher or professor says you do. No really, you need literary criticisms to help support the thesis of your research paper. By looking to what others have written, you can cite their research in quotes in your paper to give credibility to your thesis and research.

HOW?

How do I find literary criticisms?

You find literary criticisms by searching in library databases such as JSTOR, Gale Literary Resource Center, Project Muse, and others using keyword terms.

Unfortunately, literary criticisms are getting more difficult to find as more and more information is published online.

This guide is designed to start you on your research project.

Use the list of MLA style citations of literary criticisms at the back of this book to help you.

Good luck with your research project!

MLA Style Citations for Scholarly Articles, Peer-Reviewed and Critical Essays

1. "The Influence of Ernest Hemingway." *Twentieth-Century Literary Criticism*, edited by Thomas J. Schoenberg and Lawrence J. Trudeau, vol. 162, Gale, 2005. *Literature Resource Center*, go.galegroup.com/ps/i.do?p=GLS&sw=w&u=fjp_jvpl&v=2.1&it=r&id=GALE%7CH1410001404&asid=506a76688c9cc33337176d583af3aeb7. Accessed date.

2. Ako, Edward O. "Ernest Hemingway, Derek Walcott, and Old Men of the Sea." *Children's Literature Review*, edited by Jelena Krstovic, vol. 168, Gale, 2012. *Children's Literature Review Online*, go.galegroup.com/ps/i.do?p=GLS&sw=w&u=fjp_jvpl&v=2.1&it=r&id=GALE%7CYEIBSG498164136&asid=a2af4bb94c81c6e22610e5f83bd58c96. Accessed date. Originally published in *CLA Journal*, vol. 48, no. 2, Dec. 2004, pp. 200-212.

3. Allen, Charles A. "Ernest Hemingway's Clean, Well-Lighted Heros." *Short Story Criticism*, edited by Jenny Cromie, vol. 40, Gale, 2001. *Short Story Criticism Online*, go.galegroup.com/ps/i.do?p=GLS&sw=w&u=fjp_jvpl&v=2.1&it=r&id=GALE%7CSVKTQP867261212&asid=960d5f679a8f997f2ce041d1521f965a. Accessed date. Originally published in *The Pacific Spectator: A Journal of Interpretation*, vol. 9, no. 4, Autumn 1955, pp. 383-389.

4. Alshammari, Jaber Nashi M. "Analyzing Arabic translation methods of English similes: A case study of the old man and the sea by Ernest Hemingway." *Theory and Practice in Language Studies*, vol. 6, no. 3, 2016, p. 485+. *Literature Resource Center*,

go.galegroup.com/ps/i.do?p=GLS&sw=w&u=fjp_jvpl&v=2.1&it=r&id=GALE%7CA461970501&asid=30c07cf3d47e91429d644ff5ac70dcfa. Accessed date.

5. Amidon, Stephen. "Ernest Hemingway's The Sun Also Rises." *American Writers Classics*, edited by Jay Parini, vol. 1, Charles Scribner's Sons, 2003, pp. 321-337. *Scribner Writer Series*, go.galegroup.com/ps/i.do?p=GLS&sw=w&u=fjp_jvpl&v=2.1&it=r&id=GALE%7CCX1382700027&asid=01c7536b2e44585d9e0d634619414275. Accessed date.

6. Baker, Carlos. "Article by Carlos Baker." *Short Story Criticism*, edited by Laurie Lanzen Harris and Sheila Fitzgerald, vol. 1, Gale, 1988. *Short Story Criticism Online*, go.galegroup.com/ps/i.do?p=GLS&sw=w&u=fjp_jvpl&v=2.1&it=r&id=GALE%7CSWPAUP932097756&asid=5e070fde56dac4d67d9b45dd4edc9161. Accessed date. Originally published in *Hemingway: The Writer as Artist, Third Edition*, by Carlos Baker, Princeton University Press, 1963.

7. Baker, Carlos. "Hemingway's Ancient Mariner." *Short Story Criticism*, edited by Anna Sheets-Nesbitt, vol. 36, Gale, 2000. *Short Story Criticism Online*, go.galegroup.com/ps/i.do?p=GLS&sw=w&u=fjp_jvpl&v=2.1&it=r&id=GALE%7CUKTGQC258888162&asid=454b1791fa7cca82b868072340d3ff15. Accessed date. Originally published in *Ernest Hemingway: Critiques of Four Major Novels*, edited by Carlos Baker, Charles Scribner's Sons, 1962, pp. 156-172.

8. Barbour, James, and Robert Sattelmeyer. "Baseball and Baseball Talk in *The Old Man and the Sea*." *Short

Story Criticism, edited by Anna Sheets-Nesbitt, vol. 36, Gale, 2000. *Literature Resource Center*, go.galegroup.com/ps/i.do?p=GLS&sw=w&u=fjp_jvpl&v=2.1&it=r&id=GALE%7CH1420024362&asid=40abaa72ce8b03747d3118b6d01ea792. Accessed date. Originally published in *Fitzgerald/Hemingway Annual*, 1975, pp. 281-287.

9. Baskett, Sam S. "Toward a Fifth Dimension in the Old Man and the Sea." *Short Story Criticism*, edited by Anna Sheets-Nesbitt, vol. 36, Gale, 2000. *Short Story Criticism Online*, go.galegroup.com/ps/i.do?p=GLS&sw=w&u=fjp_jvpl&v=2.1&it=r&id=GALE%7CSVKKYD900034927&asid=296ff783261e99e1e23c8fc286b442df. Accessed date. Originally published in *The Centennial Review*, vol. 19, no. 4, Fall 1975, pp. 269-286.

10. Beegel, Susan F. "Santiago and the Eternal Feminine: Gendering la Mar in the Old Man and the Sea." *Children's Literature Review*, edited by Jelena Krstovic, vol. 168, Gale, 2012. *Children's Literature Review Online*, go.galegroup.com/ps/i.do?p=GLS&sw=w&u=fjp_jvpl&v=2.1&it=r&id=GALE%7CUSBBUU725414739&asid=124d4f8d7a5a67c92d0622281c17bb01. Accessed date. Originally published in *Hemingway and Women: Female Critics and the Female Voice*, edited by Lawrence R. Broer and Gloria Holland, The University of Alabama Press, 2002, pp. 131-156.

11. Beegel, Susan F. "The Monster of Cojimar: a meditation on Hemingway, sharks, and war." *The Hemingway Review*, vol. 34, no. 2, 2015, p. 9+. *Literature Resource Center*,

go.galegroup.com/ps/i.do?p=GLS&sw=w&u=fjp_jvpl&v=2.1&it=r&id=GALE%7CA412554752&asid=fc04299ec31603978b3d512236df48d2. Accessed date.

12. Bender, Bert. "Harry Burns and Professor MacWalsey in Ernest Hemingway's To Have and Have Not." *The Hemingway Review*, vol. 28, no. 1, 2008, p. 35+. *Literature Resource Center*, go.galegroup.com/ps/i.do?p=GLS&sw=w&u=fjp_jvpl&v=2.1&it=r&id=GALE%7CA191011216&asid=548e85c5e10d6d38ded18a825b8ac47b. Accessed date.

13. Bittner, John R. "'African journeys: Hemingway's influence on the life and writings of Robert Ruark'. (Articles)." *The Hemingway Review*, vol. 21, no. 2, 2002, p. 4+. *Literature Resource Center*, go.galegroup.com/ps/i.do?p=GLS&sw=w&u=fjp_jvpl&v=2.1&it=r&id=GALE%7CA87426218&asid=8a9456118b04417fcbea7328ec6596ef. Accessed date.

14. Bradford, M. E. "On the Importance of Discovering God: Faulkner and Hemingway's the Old Man and the Sea." *Children's Literature Review*, edited by Jelena Krstovic, vol. 168, Gale, 2012. *Children's Literature Review Online*, go.galegroup.com/ps/i.do?p=GLS&sw=w&u=fjp_jvpl&v=2.1&it=r&id=GALE%7CRCZKWQ251499920&asid=dbbfb8948758d16b74e56e9040238864. Accessed date. Originally published in *Mississippi Quarterly*, vol. 20, no. 3, Summer 1967, pp. 158-162.

15. Burgess, Anthony. "He Wrote Good." *Contemporary Literary Criticism*, edited by Carolyn Riley, vol. 3, Gale, 1975. *Contemporary Literary Criticism Online*, go.galegroup.com/ps/i.do?p=GLS&sw=w&u=fjp_jvpl

&v=2.1&it=r&id=GALE%7CMCGIEU866714860&asid=b86594f6c57cf4ed68d75d7336d9b06d. Accessed date. Originally published in *Urgent Copy: Literary Studies*, by Anthony Burgess, Norton, 1968, pp. 121-126.

16. Burhans, Clinton S. "The Old Man and the Sea: Hemingway's Tragic Vision of Man." *Short Story Criticism*, edited by Anna Sheets-Nesbitt, vol. 36, Gale, 2000. *Short Story Criticism Online*, go.galegroup.com/ps/i.do?p=GLS&sw=w&u=fjp_jvpl&v=2.1&it=r&id=GALE%7CQUIRFY524515827&asid=8d25dda9dc5ab899f8edfa6ee0ed10c3. Accessed date. Originally published in *American Literature*, vol. 31, no. 4, Jan. 1960, pp. 446-455.

17. Butterfield, Herbie. "Ernest Hemingway." *Contemporary Literary Criticism*, edited by Daniel G. Marowski, vol. 41, Gale, 1987. *Contemporary Literary Criticism Online*, go.galegroup.com/ps/i.do?p=GLS&sw=w&u=fjp_jvpl&v=2.1&it=r&id=GALE%7CNHGDZE294008571&asid=83a86604f885f0ed98cc1f6de173c491. Accessed date. Originally published in *American Fiction: New Readings*, edited by Richard Gray, Barnes & Noble, 1983, pp. 184-199.

18. Cain, William E. "Death Sentences: Rereading *The Old Man and the Sea*." *Children's Literature Review*, edited by Jelena Krstovic, vol. 168, Gale, 2012. *Literature Resource Center*, go.galegroup.com/ps/i.do?p=GLS&sw=w&u=fjp_jvpl&v=2.1&it=r&id=GALE%7CH1420106417&asid=a14b4951e1ba9c15dbb324858f7779b4. Accessed date.

Originally published in *Sewanee Review*, vol. 114, no. 1, Jan.-Mar. 2006, pp. 112-125.

19. Carson, David L. "Symbolism in a Farewell to Arms." *Twentieth-Century Literary Criticism*, edited by Linda Pavlovski and Scott T. Darga, vol. 115, Gale, 2002. *20th Century Literature Criticism Online*, go.galegroup.com/ps/i.do?p=GLS&sw=w&u=fjp_jvpl&v=2.1&it=r&id=GALE%7CFLTFHB109516104&asid=1237d6d6953e0db89f95f00e2449d2a0. Accessed date. Originally published in *English Studies*, vol. 53, Dec. 1972, pp. 518-522.

20. Chandarlapaty, Raj. "Through the lens of the beatniks: Norman Mailer and modern American man's quest for self-realization." *The Mailer Review*, vol. 5, no. 1, 2011, p. 231+. *Literature Resource Center*, go.galegroup.com/ps/i.do?p=GLS&sw=w&u=fjp_jvpl&v=2.1&it=r&id=GALE%7CA357759686&asid=21536cb02421a2a097193b256df3f15f. Accessed date.

21. Connolly, Cyrd. "Ernest Hemingway: 2." *Contemporary Literary Criticism*, edited by Carolyn Riley and Phyllis Carmel Mendelson, vol. 6, Gale, 1976. *Contemporary Literary Criticism Online*, go.galegroup.com/ps/i.do?p=GLS&sw=w&u=fjp_jvpl&v=2.1&it=r&id=GALE%7CXEJANS510485578&asid=088c05a996d83dba0688e472547ceccf. Accessed date. Originally published in *Previous Convictions*, by Cyrd Connolly, Hamish Hamilton, 1963, pp. 293-298.

22. Cooperman, Stanley. "Hemingway and Old Age: Santiago as Priest of Time." *Short Story Criticism*, edited by Anna Sheets-Nesbitt, vol. 36, Gale, 2000. *Literature Resource Center*,

go.galegroup.com/ps/i.do?p=GLS&sw=w&u=fjp_jvpl&v=2.1&it=r&id=GALE%7CH1420024353&asid=371077fe9f7fe9a49198b87660a15084. Accessed date. Originally published in *College English*, vol. 27, no. 3, Dec. 1965, pp. 215-220.

23. Cowley, Malcolm. "Hemingway's Novel Has the Rich Simplicity of a Classic." *Contemporary Literary Criticism*, edited by Sharon R. Gunton, vol. 19, Gale, 1981. *Contemporary Literary Criticism Online*, go.galegroup.com/ps/i.do?p=GLS&sw=w&u=fjp_jvpl&v=2.1&it=r&id=GALE%7CWTOYXR570690203&asid=dd16571cf7697ec50108631e5441a59e. Accessed date. Originally published in *The New York Herald Tribune Book Review*, 7 Sept. 1952.

24. Crocker, Michael W., and Robert C. Evans. "Faulkner's 'Barn Burning' and O'Connor's 'Everything That Rises Must Converge,'." *Contemporary Literary Criticism*, edited by Deborah A. Schmitt, vol. 104, Gale, 1998. *Literature Resource Center*, go.galegroup.com/ps/i.do?p=GLS&sw=w&u=fjp_jvpl&v=2.1&it=r&id=GALE%7CH1100001848&asid=c745c59a86a770cf68616911e3d02aa6. Accessed date. Originally published in *CLA Journal*, vol. 36, no. 4, June 1993, pp. 371-383.

25. Davis, Carl. "An overview of *The Old Man and the Sea*." *Literature Resource Center*, Gale, 2017. *Literature Resource Center*, go.galegroup.com/ps/i.do?p=GLS&sw=w&u=fjp_jvpl&v=2.1&it=r&id=GALE%7CH1420006109&asid=e1275e9b51755deb82403e63eb0b0596. Accessed date.

26. Donaldson, Scott. "Ernest (Miller) Hemingway." *American Writers, Retrospective Supplement 1*, edited by A. Walton Litz and Molly Weigel, Charles Scribner's Sons, 1998. *Literature Resource Center*, go.galegroup.com/ps/i.do?p=GLS&sw=w&u=fjp_jvpl&v=2.1&it=r&id=GALE%7CH1479001547&asid=c1e492b17c14db760fba595b8ca70568. Accessed date.

27. Donaldson, Scott. "Hemingway, Ernest 1899—1961." *American Writers, Retrospective Supplement 1*, edited by A. Walton Litz and Molly Weigel, Charles Scribner's Sons, 1998, pp. 169-191. *Scribner Writer Series*, go.galegroup.com/ps/i.do?p=GLS&sw=w&u=fjp_jvpl&v=2.1&it=r&id=GALE%7CCX1380200017&asid=a1c7809c41507aa75e357283099c66cf. Accessed date.

28. Eddins, Dwight. "Of rocks and marlin: the existentialist agon in Camus's the myth of sisyphus and hemingway's the old man and the sea. (Articles)." *The Hemingway Review*, vol. 21, no. 1, 2001, p. 68+. *Literature Resource Center*, go.galegroup.com/ps/i.do?p=GLS&sw=w&u=fjp_jvpl&v=2.1&it=r&id=GALE%7CA80805141&asid=fdd51fbc55e0187a07e8b3cc25e02f77. Accessed date.

29. Flora, Joseph M. "Biblical Allusion in the Old Man and the Sea." *Short Story Criticism*, edited by Anna Sheets-Nesbitt, vol. 36, Gale, 2000. *Short Story Criticism Online*, go.galegroup.com/ps/i.do?p=GLS&sw=w&u=fjp_jvpl&v=2.1&it=r&id=GALE%7CXUWNQQ854552725&asid=69374f9ced6676109db614549584de2b. Accessed date. Originally published in *Studies in*

Short Fiction, vol. 10, no. 2, Spring 1973, pp. 143-147.

30. Florczyk, Steven. "Hemingway's 'Tragic Adventure': Angling for Peace in the Natural Landscape of the Fisherman." *Short Story Criticism*, edited by Lawrence J. Trudeau, vol. 189, Gale, 2014. *Short Story Criticism Online*, go.galegroup.com/ps/i.do?p=GLS&sw=w&u=fjp_jvpl&v=2.1&it=r&id=GALE%7CTHFIWG911179882&asid=00cddc92307589c99d11a40b686e88d2. Accessed date. Originally published in *North Dakota Quarterly*, vol. 68, no. 2-3, 2001, pp. 156-165.

31. Friedman, Norman. "Harry or Ernest? The Unresolved Ambiguity in 'The Snows of Kilimanjaro'." *Short Story Criticism*, edited by Lawrence J. Trudeau, vol. 212, Gale, 2015. *Literature Resource Center*, go.galegroup.com/ps/i.do?p=GLS&sw=w&u=fjp_jvpl&v=2.1&it=r&id=GALE%7CH1420119609&asid=711f8bc1798b147ed0c3353328f17d19. Accessed date. Originally published in *Creative and Critical Approaches to the Short Story*, edited by Noel Harold Kaylor, Jr., Mellen, 1997, pp. 359-373.

32. Frohock, W. M. "Ernest Hemingway—The River and the Hawk." *Contemporary Literary Criticism*, edited by Carolyn Riley, vol. 1, Gale, 1973. *Contemporary Literary Criticism Online*, go.galegroup.com/ps/i.do?p=GLS&sw=w&u=fjp_jvpl&v=2.1&it=r&id=GALE%7CEJQYPS847907372&asid=4e694ae0b9c175fda107da9547830650. Accessed date. Originally published in *The Novel of Violence in America*, by W. M. Frohock, Southern Methodist University Press, 1957, pp. 166-198.

33. Glenday, Michael K. "Some Versions of Real: The Novellas of Saul Bellow." *Short Story Criticism*, edited by David L. Siegel, vol. 14, Gale, 1994. *Short Story Criticism Online*, go.galegroup.com/ps/i.do?p=GLS&sw=w&u=fjp_jvpl&v=2.1&it=r&id=GALE%7CNPBJUK767650161&asid=6781a362081231671a8109d7de411e37. Accessed date. Originally published in *The Modern American Novella*, edited by A. Robert Lee, Vision Press, 1989, pp. 162-177.

34. Graham, John. "Ernest Hemingway: The Meaning of Style." *Contemporary Literary Criticism*, edited by Carolyn Riley, vol. 3, Gale, 1975. *Contemporary Literary Criticism Online*, go.galegroup.com/ps/i.do?p=GLS&sw=w&u=fjp_jvpl&v=2.1&it=r&id=GALE%7CHEUABA475164038&asid=e1ec68bd0b4757ce3e7cde771e5b0367. Accessed date. Originally published in *Studies in A Farewell to Arms*, edited by John Graham, Merrill, 1971, pp. 97-98.

35. Grebstein, Sheldon Norman. "Hemingway's Craft in the Old Man and the Sea." *Short Story Criticism*, edited by Anna Sheets-Nesbitt, vol. 36, Gale, 2000. *Short Story Criticism Online*, go.galegroup.com/ps/i.do?p=GLS&sw=w&u=fjp_jvpl&v=2.1&it=r&id=GALE%7CYINBTU390972946&asid=5372d4b1344b2b85f6ce0d8876a2286c. Accessed date. Originally published in *The Fifties: Fiction, Poetry, Drama*, edited by Warren French, Everett/Edwards, Inc., pp. 41-50.

36. Guttmann, Allen. "Mechanized Doom: Ernest Hemingway and the Spanish Civil War." *Twentieth-

Century Literary Criticism, edited by Dennis Poupard, vol. 26, Gale, 1988. *20th Century Literature Criticism Online*, go.galegroup.com/ps/i.do?p=GLS&sw=w&u=fjp_jvpl&v=2.1&it=r&id=GALE%7CJGPXYN784070383&asid=20ceb9c8e35b375674f6d9fd1a28b884. Accessed date. Originally published in *The Massachusetts Review*, vol. 1, no. 3, May 1960, pp. 541-561.

37. Hamilton, John Bowen. "Hemingway and the Christian Paradox." *Short Story Criticism*, edited by Anna Sheets-Nesbitt, vol. 36, Gale, 2000. *Literature Resource Center*, go.galegroup.com/ps/i.do?p=GLS&sw=w&u=fjp_jvpl&v=2.1&it=r&id=GALE%7CH1420024359&asid=0b9af5eb7227182ee5d84a8824bca484. Accessed date. Originally published in *Renascence: Essays on Values in Literature*, vol. 24, no. 3, Spring 1972, pp. 141-154.

38. Handy, William J. "A New Dimension for a Hero: Santiago of *The Old Man and the Sea*." *Contemporary Literary Criticism Select*, Gale, 2008. *Literature Resource Center*, go.galegroup.com/ps/i.do?p=GLS&sw=w&u=fjp_jvpl&v=2.1&it=r&id=GALE%7CH1100000403&asid=904ad2d221284dc0f7e2238fedd8943f. Accessed date. Originally published in *Contemporary Novels, The University of Texas*, 1962, pp. 62-69.

39. Hemingway, Ernest. "Article by Ernest Hemingway." *Nineteenth-Century Literature Criticism*, edited by Laurie Lanzen Harris and Jay Parini, vol. 12, Gale, 1986. *19th Century Literature Criticism Online*, go.galegroup.com/ps/i.do?p=GLS&sw=w&u=fjp_jvpl

&v=2.1&it=r&id=GALE%7CCEXCVM618788850&asid=e4e35bb84476c1135f0d0ecbb4240699. Accessed date. Originally published in *Green Hills of Africa*, by Ernest Hemingway, Charles Scribner's Sons, 1935.

40. Herlihy, Jeffrey. "Eyes the Same Color As the Sea: Santiago's Expatriation from Spain and Ethnic Otherness in Hemingway's the Old Man and the Sea." *Children's Literature Review*, edited by Jelena Krstovic, vol. 168, Gale, 2012. *Children's Literature Review Online*, go.galegroup.com/ps/i.do?p=GLS&sw=w&u=fjp_jvpl&v=2.1&it=r&id=GALE%7CSUXLKK169113288&asid=dcb6adc75ed479c4fa11f96a4e61218e. Accessed date. Originally published in *Hemingway Review*, vol. 28, no. 2, Spring 2009, pp. 25-44.

41. Herlihy-Mera, Jeffrey. "Cuba in Hemingway." *The Hemingway Review*, vol. 36, no. 2, 2017, p. 8+. *Literature Resource Center*, go.galegroup.com/ps/i.do?p=GLS&sw=w&u=fjp_jvpl&v=2.1&it=r&id=GALE%7CA493462195&asid=3fcd03d8cc306152bdadcd24d95d8840. Accessed date.

42. Hertzel, Leo J. "The Look of Religion: Hemingway and Catholicism." *Twentieth-Century Literary Criticism*, edited by Linda Pavlovski and Scott T. Darga, vol. 110, Gale, 2001. *20th Century Literature Criticism Online*, go.galegroup.com/ps/i.do?p=GLS&sw=w&u=fjp_jvpl&v=2.1&it=r&id=GALE%7CCIHLGX496384827&asid=b079461f422bee7ad5295c7c909ed53f. Accessed date. Originally published in *Renascence*, vol. 17, no. 2, Winter 1964, pp. 77-81.

43. Hicks, Granville. "Hemingway: The Complexities That Animated the Man." *Twentieth-Century Literary Criticism*, edited by Janet Witalec, vol. 119, Gale, 2002. *20th Century Literature Criticism Online*, go.galegroup.com/ps/i.do?p=GLS&sw=w&u=fjp_jvpl&v=2.1&it=r&id=GALE%7CGTSZRD223837212&asid=991b4c12404f7888f169dea797a4185b. Accessed date. Originally published in *Saturday Review of Literature*, vol. 52, no. 16, 19 Apr. 1969, pp. 31-33.

44. Hofling, Charles K. "Hemingway's *The Old Man and the Sea* and the Male Reader." *Short Story Criticism*, edited by Anna Sheets-Nesbitt, vol. 36, Gale, 2000. *Literature Resource Center*, go.galegroup.com/ps/i.do?p=GLS&sw=w&u=fjp_jvpl&v=2.1&it=r&id=GALE%7CH1420024352&asid=0932022250a8266502e2d1015e63c0b2. Accessed date. Originally published in *The American Imago*, vol. 20, no. 2, Summer 1963, pp. 161-173.

45. Hollenberg, Alexander. "The spacious foreground: interpreting simplicity and ecocritical ethics in The Old Man and the Sea." *The Hemingway Review*, vol. 31, no. 2, 2012, p. 27+. *Literature Resource Center*, go.galegroup.com/ps/i.do?p=GLS&sw=w&u=fjp_jvpl&v=2.1&it=r&id=GALE%7CA293352492&asid=806d4e29c9ab42ebfaf1433a41ec62b8. Accessed date.

46. Hovey, Richard B. "The Old Man and the Sea: A New Heming Way Hero." *Short Story Criticism*, edited by Anna Sheets-Nesbitt, vol. 36, Gale, 2000. *Short Story Criticism Online*, go.galegroup.com/ps/i.do?p=GLS&sw=w&u=fjp_jvpl&v=2.1&it=r&id=GALE%7CVWGNVC683396330&asid=386b052cc179870535536e3c0e2cb25e.

Accessed date. Originally published in *Discourse: A Review of the Liberal Arts*, vol. 9, no. 3, Summer 1966, pp. 283-294.

47. Hurley, C. Harold. "Baseball in Hemingway's 'The Three-Day Blow': the way it really was in the fall of 1916." *The Hemingway Review*, vol. 16, no. 1, 1996, p. 43+. *Literature Resource Center*, go.galegroup.com/ps/i.do?p=GLS&sw=w&u=fjp_jvpl&v=2.1&it=r&id=GALE%7CA18963166&asid=34f642ab7f365a5e638020f9ce9fdf2c. Accessed date.

48. Hurley, C. Harold. "The Facts Behind the Fiction: The 1950 American League Pennant Race and the Old Man and the Sea." *Twentieth-Century Literary Criticism*, edited by Jennifer Baise, vol. 86, Gale, 2000. *20th Century Literature Criticism Online*, go.galegroup.com/ps/i.do?p=GLS&sw=w&u=fjp_jvpl&v=2.1&it=r&id=GALE%7CGPUWJM371149999&asid=baa12d709a672ed338984bc1c512b451. Accessed date. Originally published in *Hemingway's Debt to Baseball in The Old Man and the Sea, The Edwin*, Mellen Press, 1992, pp. 77-93.

49. Kakutani, Michiko. "Hemingway at Sunset." *Contemporary Literary Criticism*, edited by Daniel G. Marowski, vol. 41, Gale, 1987. *Contemporary Literary Criticism Online*, go.galegroup.com/ps/i.do?p=GLS&sw=w&u=fjp_jvpl&v=2.1&it=r&id=GALE%7CCNFYKU171023588&asid=7d1e868f055ac4525f2558deb44a9adb. Accessed date. Originally published in *The New York Times*, 1 June 1985.

50. Lindsay, Creighton. "Hemingway's Nexus of Pastoral and Tragedy." *Short Story Criticism*, edited by Janet Witalec, vol. 63, Gale, 2004. *Literature Resource Center*, go.galegroup.com/ps/i.do?p=GLS&sw=w&u=fjp_jvpl&v=2.1&it=r&id=GALE%7CH1420052531&asid=cf270179b62bfe3bad42b9a9a7857c57. Accessed date. Originally published in *CLA Journal*, vol. 43, no. 4, June 2000, pp. 454-478.

51. Listoe, Daniel. "Writing toward Death: The Stylistic Necessities of the Last Journeys of Ernest Hemingway." *Twentieth-Century Literary Criticism*, edited by Thomas J. Schoenberg, vol. 203, Gale, 2008. *Literature Resource Center*, go.galegroup.com/ps/i.do?p=GLS&sw=w&u=fjp_jvpl&v=2.1&it=r&id=GALE%7CH1420083002&asid=bc16511627c58c6db88d9c77b669b43e. Accessed date. Originally published in *North Dakota Quarterly*, vol. 64, no. 3, 1997, pp. 89-95.

52. Llosa, Mario Vargas. "Extemporaneities." *Twentieth-Century Literary Criticism*, edited by Thomas J. Schoenberg and Lawrence J. Trudeau, vol. 162, Gale, 2005. *Literature Resource Center*, go.galegroup.com/ps/i.do?p=GLS&sw=w&u=fjp_jvpl&v=2.1&it=r&id=GALE%7CH1420064858&asid=c6f891ef4d2976af342bfefcce1e44b7. Accessed date. Originally published in *Salmagundi*, no. 128-129, Fall-Winter 2000, pp. 42-47.

53. Losada, Luis A. "George Sisler, Manolin's age, and Hemingway's use of baseball." *The Hemingway Review*, vol. 14, no. 1, 1994, p. 79+. *Literature Resource Center*,

go.galegroup.com/ps/i.do?p=GLS&sw=w&u=fjp_jvpl&v=2.1&it=r&id=GALE%7CA16114361&asid=b7de85c197ee7f60c66baa145d19f9b4. Accessed date.

54. Love, Glen A. "Hemingway among the Animals." *Twentieth-Century Literary Criticism*, edited by Thomas J. Schoenberg and Lawrence J. Trudeau, vol. 162, Gale, 2005. *20th Century Literature Criticism Online*, go.galegroup.com/ps/i.do?p=GLS&sw=w&u=fjp_jvpl&v=2.1&it=r&id=GALE%7CJUPUTH919345209&asid=2ea67035ffcf2001c9fb6ccd1f83f54b. Accessed date. Originally published in *Practical Ecocriticism: Literature, Biology and the Environment*, University of Virginia Press, 2003, pp. 117-181.

55. Luis, William. "Lunes De Revolución: Literature and Culture in the First Years of the Cuban Revolution." *Guillermo Cabrera Infante*: *Assays, Essays and Other Arts*, by Ardis L. Nelson, Twayne Publishers, 1999, pp. 16-38. *Twayne's Authors Series*, go.galegroup.com/ps/i.do?p=GLS&sw=w&u=fjp_jvpl&v=2.1&it=r&id=GALE%7CCX1598500014&asid=6d14c2b029f6223930db474bf4d4bea0. Accessed date.

56. MacDonald, Scott. "Implications of Narrative Perspective in Hemingway's 'The Undefeated'." *Short Story Criticism*, edited by Lawrence J. Trudeau, vol. 244, Gale, 2017. *Literature Resource Center*, go.galegroup.com/ps/i.do?p=GLS&sw=w&u=fjp_jvpl&v=2.1&it=r&id=GALE%7CH1420123334&asid=71501f206753674a7fd83f4a6a6660aa. Accessed date. Originally published in *Journal of Narrative Technique*, vol. 2, no. 1, 1972, pp. 1-15.

57. Marcus, Phillip L. "I knew that underneath Mr. H and I were really a lot alike': reading Hemingway's The Old Man and the Sea with Elizabeth Bishop's 'The Fish." *The Hemingway Review*, vol. 33, no. 1, 2013, p. 27+. *Literature Resource Center*, go.galegroup.com/ps/i.do?p=GLS&sw=w&u=fjp_jvpl&v=2.1&it=r&id=GALE%7CA357261587&asid=ea037ed5ea6812a30502866200126a26. Accessed date.

58. Meinke, Peter. "Swallowing America Whole." *Contemporary Literary Criticism*, edited by Carolyn Riley, vol. 4, Gale, 1975. *Contemporary Literary Criticism Online*, go.galegroup.com/ps/i.do?p=GLS&sw=w&u=fjp_jvpl&v=2.1&it=r&id=GALE%7CHNUFYL292473715&asid=a54c22dd2a00674534124a5ae603f797. Accessed date. Originally published in *The New Republic*, 22 Sept. 1973, pp. 28-31.

59. Melling, Philip. "Cultural imperialism, Afro-Cuban religion, and Santiago's failure in Hemingway's The Old Man and the Sea." *The Hemingway Review*, vol. 26, no. 1, 2006, p. 6+. *Literature Resource Center*, go.galegroup.com/ps/i.do?p=GLS&sw=w&u=fjp_jvpl&v=2.1&it=r&id=GALE%7CA155918659&asid=4cadfd194b1204d1ff7f774eca1c13de. Accessed date.

60. MEYER, WILLIAM E.H., JR. "Faulkner, Hemingway, et al.: The Emersonian Test of American Authorship." *The Mississippi Quarterly*, vol. 51, no. 3, 1998, p. 557. *Literature Resource Center*, go.galegroup.com/ps/i.do?p=GLS&sw=w&u=fjp_jvpl&v=2.1&it=r&id=GALE%7CA54273196&asid=23796f4e5305f26728e558d46e90e22f. Accessed date.

61. MILLER, PAUL W. "HEMINGWAY VS. STENDHAL, OR PAPA'S LAST FIGHT WITH A DEAD WRITER." *The Hemingway Review*, vol. 19, no. 1, 1999, p. 127. *Literature Resource Center*, go.galegroup.com/ps/i.do?p=GLS&sw=w&u=fjp_jvpl&v=2.1&it=r&id=GALE%7CA58243542&asid=83fe8c5075723db095a465d29a300438. Accessed date.

62. Milson, Menahem. "A Great 20th-Century Novelist." *Contemporary Literary Criticism*, edited by Jeffrey W. Hunter, vol. 153, Gale, 2002. *Contemporary Literary Criticism Online*, go.galegroup.com/ps/i.do?p=GLS&sw=w&u=fjp_jvpl&v=2.1&it=r&id=GALE%7CMZETYP339078999&asid=727ea2f642dabb7b83e0639e704a56cd. Accessed date. Originally published in *Commentary*, vol. 91, no. 6, June 1991, pp. 34-38.

63. Morgan, Kathleen, and Luis Losada. "Santiago in the Old Man and the Sea: A Homeric Hero." *Twentieth-Century Literary Criticism*, edited by Jennifer Baise, vol. 82, Gale, 1999. *20th Century Literature Criticism Online*, go.galegroup.com/ps/i.do?p=GLS&sw=w&u=fjp_jvpl&v=2.1&it=r&id=GALE%7CMDGFUW731346936&asid=83f305bb13c46b44a8e9686c87563256. Accessed date. Originally published in *The Hemingway Review*, vol. 12, no. 1, Fall 1992, pp. 35-51.

64. Murphy, John. "Unspoken Depths in the Old Man and the Sea." *Children's Literature Review*, edited by Jelena Krstovic, vol. 168, Gale, 2012. *Children's Literature Review Online*, go.galegroup.com/ps/i.do?p=GLS&sw=w&u=fjp_jvpl

&v=2.1&it=r&id=GALE%7CYSGRLU796402423&asid=0a85d313cf7c584108b419a38ad0f225. Accessed date. Originally published in *CEA Forum*, vol. 18, no. 2-4, 1988, pp. 18-20.

65. Oberhelman, Harley D. "Hemingway and García Márquez: Two Shipwreck Narratives." *Children's Literature Review*, edited by Jelena Krstovic, vol. 168, Gale, 2012. *Children's Literature Review Online*, go.galegroup.com/ps/i.do?p=GLS&sw=w&u=fjp_jvpl&v=2.1&it=r&id=GALE%7CPFIBXY802964619&asid=87d065ff66e28c3ee0cc024110e524b8. Accessed date. Originally published in *International Fiction Review*, vol. 21, no. 1-2, 1994, pp. 1-6.

66. O'Faolain, Sean. "Ernest Hemingway: Men Without Memories." *Short Story Criticism*, edited by Laurie Lanzen Harris and Sheila Fitzgerald, vol. 1, Gale, 1988. *Short Story Criticism Online*, go.galegroup.com/ps/i.do?p=GLS&sw=w&u=fjp_jvpl&v=2.1&it=r&id=GALE%7CSGAACE553115816&asid=e3d5aedd61822b103ca1ad43f0cc5de1. Accessed date. Originally published in *The Vanishing Hero: Studies in Novelists of the Twenties*, by Sean O'Faolain, 1956.

67. Ott, Mark P. "Hemingway's Hawaiian honeymoon." *The Hemingway Review*, vol. 17, no. 1, 1997, p. 58+. *Literature Resource Center*, go.galegroup.com/ps/i.do?p=GLS&sw=w&u=fjp_jvpl&v=2.1&it=r&id=GALE%7CA20181963&asid=dd6a7dcbdaecd189ad24934fb06f2f6c. Accessed date.

68. Pavloska, Susanna. "Hemingway's Primal Scene." *Twentieth-Century Literary Criticism*, edited

by Thomas J. Schoenberg, vol. 203, Gale, 2008. *Literature Resource Center*, go.galegroup.com/ps/i.do?p=GLS&sw=w&u=fjp_jvpl&v=2.1&it=r&id=GALE%7CH1420083006&asid=644a6c968731228791f5ef58c4d2822a. Accessed date. Originally published in *Modern Primitives: Race and Language in Gertrude Stein, Ernest Hemingway, and Zora Neale Hurston*, Garland Publishing, Inc., 2000, pp. 55-73.

69. Phillips, Steven R. "Hemingway and the Bullfight: The Archetypes of Tragedy." *Contemporary Literary Criticism*, edited by Carolyn Riley, vol. 3, Gale, 1975. *Contemporary Literary Criticism Online*, go.galegroup.com/ps/i.do?p=GLS&sw=w&u=fjp_jvpl&v=2.1&it=r&id=GALE%7CXCHGKG202436288&asid=eee113b1f31c4b0e26ed73a41d8cfc58. Accessed date. Originally published in *Arizona Quarterly*, Spring 1973, pp. 37-56.

70. Plath, James. "Santiago at the plate: baseball in 'The Old Man and the Sea.'(protagonist of Ernest Hemingway's novel)." *The Hemingway Review*, vol. 16, no. 1, 1996, p. 65+. *Literature Resource Center*, go.galegroup.com/ps/i.do?p=GLS&sw=w&u=fjp_jvpl&v=2.1&it=r&id=GALE%7CA18963168&asid=205af7745bff3b670ef5e6bba0e7fd8a. Accessed date.

71. Plath, James. "Shadow Rider: The Hemingway Hero As Western Archetype." *Twentieth-Century Literary Criticism*, edited by Thomas J. Schoenberg, vol. 203, Gale, 2008. *20th Century Literature Criticism Online*, go.galegroup.com/ps/i.do?p=GLS&sw=w&u=fjp_jvpl&v=2.1&it=r&id=GALE%7CGWSELB293618340&asid=42e280d4a4aea99eaef2122ecdbb7043. Accessed

date. Originally published in *Hemingway and the Natural World*, edited by Robert E. Fleming, University of Idaho Press, 1999, pp. 69-86.

72. Pratt, John Clark. "My pilgrimage: fishing for religion with Hemingway. (Articles)." *The Hemingway Review*, vol. 21, no. 1, 2001, p. 78+. *Literature Resource Center*, go.galegroup.com/ps/i.do?p=GLS&sw=w&u=fjp_jvpl&v=2.1&it=r&id=GALE%7CA80805142&asid=496c5c6dc7e4aad325b89bea9ab56aeb. Accessed date.

73. Pratt, John Clark. "My pilgrimage: fishing for religion with Hemingway. (Articles)." *The Hemingway Review*, vol. 21, no. 1, 2001, p. 78+. *Literature Resource Center*, go.galegroup.com/ps/i.do?p=GLS&sw=w&u=fjp_jvpl&v=2.1&it=r&id=GALE%7CA80805142&asid=496c5c6dc7e4aad325b89bea9ab56aeb. Accessed date.

74. Rahv, Philip. "Hemingway in the Early 1950's (1952)." *Contemporary Literary Criticism*, edited by Carolyn Riley, vol. 3, Gale, 1975. *Contemporary Literary Criticism Online*, go.galegroup.com/ps/i.do?p=GLS&sw=w&u=fjp_jvpl&v=2.1&it=r&id=GALE%7CKKLRSR756270417&asid=2841ed1ab761af64c4dbd0568f987f7c. Accessed date. Originally published in *The Myth and the Powerhouse*, by Philip Rahv, Farrar, Straus, 1965, pp. 198-201.

75. Reynolds, Michael. "Ringing the Changes: Hemingway's Bell Tolls Fifty." *Contemporary Literary Criticism*, edited by James P. Draper and Jennifer Allison Brostrom, vol. 80, Gale,

1994. *Contemporary Literary Criticism Online*, go.galegroup.com/ps/i.do?p=GLS&sw=w&u=fjp_jvpl&v=2.1&it=r&id=GALE%7CMIQTHA650952177&asid=f3bc54d42776708572bd8b9167ed54b5. Accessed date. Originally published in *The Virginia Quarterly Review*, vol. 67, no. 1, Winter 1991, pp. 1-18.

76. Samuels, Charles Thomas. "The Heresy of Self-Love." *Twentieth-Century Literary Criticism*, edited by Janet Witalec, vol. 119, Gale, 2002. *20th Century Literature Criticism Online*, go.galegroup.com/ps/i.do?p=GLS&sw=w&u=fjp_jvpl&v=2.1&it=r&id=GALE%7CFUFBVI262303690&asid=e8a4503c8c7728fd9442ceb072dc1836. Accessed date. Originally published in *New Republic*, vol. 160, no. 2835, 26 Apr. 1969, pp. 28-32.

77. Sanderson, Stewart F. "Ernest Hemingway: Overview." *Reference Guide to American Literature*, edited by Jim Kamp, 3rd ed., St. James Press, 1994. *Literature Resource Center*, go.galegroup.com/ps/i.do?p=GLS&sw=w&u=fjp_jvpl&v=2.1&it=r&id=GALE%7CH1420003894&asid=6a3d4a6c33b8a7b59334755a011ab8e4. Accessed date.

78. Schorer, Mark. "With Grace Under Pressure." *Short Story Criticism*, edited by Anna Sheets-Nesbitt, vol. 36, Gale, 2000. *Short Story Criticism Online*, go.galegroup.com/ps/i.do?p=GLS&sw=w&u=fjp_jvpl&v=2.1&it=r&id=GALE%7CZCWNBZ688614299&asid=dd905bb4afc07b5913d296f7c6f9e811. Accessed date. Originally published in *Ernest Hemingway: Critiques of Four Major Novels*, edited by Carlos Baker, Charles Scribner's Sons, 1962, pp. 132-134.

79. Sharei, Vahideh. "A comparative study of the strategies employed in 'The Old Man and the Sea' translated from English into Persian on the basis of Vinay and Darbelnet's model." *Theory and Practice in Language Studies*, vol. 7, no. 4, 2017, p. 281+. *Literature Resource Center*, go.galegroup.com/ps/i.do?p=GLS&sw=w&u=fjp_jvpl&v=2.1&it=r&id=GALE%7CA491033042&asid=c52ca4272b68725a9d37afa3d7c8b029. Accessed date.

80. Stein, William Bysshe. "Ritual in Hemingway's 'Big Two-Hearted River'." *Short Story Criticism*, edited by Lawrence J. Trudeau, vol. 189, Gale, 2014. *Literature Resource Center*, go.galegroup.com/ps/i.do?p=GLS&sw=w&u=fjp_jvpl&v=2.1&it=r&id=GALE%7CH1420116662&asid=338aa44a60b5d80c2fc2589ff64114b1. Accessed date. Originally published in *Texas Studies in Literature and Language*, vol. 1, no. 4, 1960, pp. 555-561.

81. Stephens, Gregory, and Janice Cools. "'Out too far': half-fish, beaten men, and the tenor of masculine grace in The Old Man and the Sea." *The Hemingway Review*, vol. 32, no. 2, 2013, p. 77+. *Literature Resource Center*, go.galegroup.com/ps/i.do?p=GLS&sw=w&u=fjp_jvpl&v=2.1&it=r&id=GALE%7CA338778553&asid=f12fa2a4b24fee4d63c7369376323a10. Accessed date.

82. Stephens, Robert O. "Hemingway's Old Man and the Iceberg." *Short Story Criticism*, edited by Anna Sheets-Nesbitt, vol. 36, Gale, 2000. *Short Story Criticism Online*, go.galegroup.com/ps/i.do?p=GLS&sw=w&u=fjp_jvpl&v=2.1&it=r&id=GALE%7CYEZQDO161447967&a

sid=d4d96943296f967811a0cf342b12102e. Accessed date. Originally published in *Modern Fiction Studies*, vol. 7, no. 4, Winter 1961, pp. 295-304.

83. Stoltzfus, Ben. "Article by Ben Stoltzfus." *Contemporary Literary Criticism*, edited by Dedria Bryfonski, vol. 13, Gale, 1980. *Contemporary Literary Criticism Online*, go.galegroup.com/ps/i.do?p=GLS&sw=w&u=fjp_jvpl&v=2.1&it=r&id=GALE%7CZUMRVZ049309733&asid=89412e4253abd6c824d084ad640ada8f. Accessed date. Originally published in *Gide and Hemingway: Rebels Against God*, by Ben Stoltzfus, Kennikat, 1978.

84. Stone, Robert, et al. "On Hemingway and His Influence: Conversations with Writers." *Twentieth-Century Literary Criticism*, edited by Thomas J. Schoenberg and Lawrence J. Trudeau, vol. 162, Gale, 2005. *Literature Resource Center*, go.galegroup.com/ps/i.do?p=GLS&sw=w&u=fjp_jvpl&v=2.1&it=r&id=GALE%7CH1420064856&asid=5e1d7fb7c15cf306c06464a39d6a4a6d. Accessed date. Originally published in *The Hemingway Review*, vol. 18, no. 2, Spring 1999, pp. 115-132.

85. Strychacz, Thomas. "The Self Offstage: Big Two-Hearted River and the Old Man and the Sea." *Short Story Criticism*, edited by Jelena O. Krstovic, vol. 117, Gale, 2009. *Short Story Criticism Online*, go.galegroup.com/ps/i.do?p=GLS&sw=w&u=fjp_jvpl&v=2.1&it=r&id=GALE%7CZEGGDD465440602&asid=d3c4ee08da65fc1ee0fed182bdcf72c7. Accessed date. Originally published in *Hemingway's Theaters of*

Masculinity, Louisiana State University Press, 2003, pp. 221-258.

86. Strychacz, Thomas. "Unraveling the Masculine Ethos in 'The Short Happy Life of Francis Macomber.'." *Short Story Criticism*, edited by Jelena O. Krstovic, vol. 137, Gale, 2010. *Literature Resource Center*, go.galegroup.com/ps/i.do?p=GLS&sw=w&u=fjp_jvpl&v=2.1&it=r&id=GALE%7CH1420099230&asid=d06222ed6db84eddd50ea757efc98435. Accessed date. Originally published in *Hemingway's Theaters of Masculinity*, Louisiana State University Press, 2003, pp. 14-52.

87. Summerhayes, Don. "Fish Story: Ways of Telling in Big Two-Hearted River." *Short Story Criticism*, edited by Janet Witalec, vol. 63, Gale, 2004. *Short Story Criticism Online*, go.galegroup.com/ps/i.do?p=GLS&sw=w&u=fjp_jvpl&v=2.1&it=r&id=GALE%7CVGVCMK715477366&asid=c0fb39101cb3e6909323851bd4a1f330. Accessed date. Originally published in *The Hemingway Review*, vol. 15, no. 1, Fall 1995, pp. 10-26.

88. Svensson, Ove G. "Ernest Hemingway and the Nobel Prize for Literature." *The Hemingway Review*, vol. 27, no. 2, 2008, p. 118+. *Literature Resource Center*, go.galegroup.com/ps/i.do?p=GLS&sw=w&u=fjp_jvpl&v=2.1&it=r&id=GALE%7CA182525100&asid=a13227b11218adf2673958afba8b558c. Accessed date.

89. Sylvester, Bickford. "Hemingway's Extended Vision: The Old Man and the Sea." *Short Story Criticism*, edited by Laurie Lanzen Harris and Sheila Fitzgerald,

vol. 1, Gale, 1988. *Short Story Criticism Online*, go.galegroup.com/ps/i.do?p=GLS&sw=w&u=fjp_jvpl&v=2.1&it=r&id=GALE%7CRJCNXN303669643&asid=9e67a675a925c147df7aff6a4c076efa. Accessed date. Originally published in *PMLA, 81*, vol. 81, no. 1, Mar. 1986, pp. 130-138.

90. Taylor, Charles. "The Old Man and the Sea: A Nietzschean Tragic Vision." *Short Story Criticism*, edited by Anna Sheets-Nesbitt, vol. 36, Gale, 2000. *Short Story Criticism Online*, go.galegroup.com/ps/i.do?p=GLS&sw=w&u=fjp_jvpl&v=2.1&it=r&id=GALE%7CPMXTKI948058001&asid=5d11031ec32f7988d57c4e9cbcc3dffa. Accessed date. Originally published in *Dalhousie Review*, vol. 61, no. 4, Winter 1981, pp. 631-643.

91. Tsuruta, Kinya. "The Twilight Years, East and West: Hemingway's *The Old Man and the Sea* and Kawabata's *The Sound of the Mountain*." *Contemporary Literary Criticism Select*, Gale, 2008. *Literature Resource Center*, go.galegroup.com/ps/i.do?p=GLS&sw=w&u=fjp_jvpl&v=2.1&it=r&id=GALE%7CH1100002363&asid=c0e38e66003331a4244cd45e841fba07. Accessed date. Originally published in *Explorations*, edited by Makoto Ueda, University Press of America, 1986, pp. 87-99.

92. Tuttleton, James W. "American Manhood and the Literature of Adventure." *Twentieth-Century Literary Criticism*, edited by Thomas J. Schoenberg and Lawrence J. Trudeau, vol. 202, Gale, 2008. *20th Century Literature Criticism Online*, go.galegroup.com/ps/i.do?p=GLS&sw=w&u=fjp_jvpl

&v=2.1&it=r&id=GALE%7CJUNGBY226581719&asid=40139a70ce274e092c27e135bef13e11. Accessed date. Originally published in *Vital Signs: Essays on American Literature and Criticism*, Ivan R. Dee, 1996, pp. 26-41.

93. Twomey, Lisa A. "Taboo or tolerable?: Hemingway's For Whom The Bell Tolls in postwar Spain." *The Hemingway Review*, vol. 30, no. 2, 2011, p. 54+. *Literature Resource Center*, go.galegroup.com/ps/i.do?p=GLS&sw=w&u=fjp_jvpl&v=2.1&it=r&id=GALE%7CA260691288&asid=90ce84349f66a41487db7a87f69210d1. Accessed date.

94. Voeller, Carey. "He Only Looked Sad the Same Way I Felt: The Textual Confessions of Hemingway's Hunters." *Short Story Criticism*, edited by Jelena O. Krstovic, vol. 137, Gale, 2010. *Short Story Criticism Online*, go.galegroup.com/ps/i.do?p=GLS&sw=w&u=fjp_jvpl&v=2.1&it=r&id=GALE%7CPYVKWX928043515&asid=1d684d2c1bae67d6f6ee211b81b3f101. Accessed date. Originally published in *Hemingway Review*, vol. 25, no. 1, Fall 2005, pp. 63-76.

95. Vowles, Richard B. "Martin A. Hansen and the Uses of the Past." *Twentieth-Century Literary Criticism*, edited by Paula Kepos, vol. 32, Gale, 1989. *20th Century Literature Criticism Online*, go.galegroup.com/ps/i.do?p=GLS&sw=w&u=fjp_jvpl&v=2.1&it=r&id=GALE%7CGXNHRJ112973893&asid=2402647694b5fed575a66f8e97a4ee53. Accessed date. Originally published in *The American-Scandinavian Review*, vol. 46, no. 1, Mar. 1958, pp. 33-40.

96. Waggoner, Eric. "Inside the current: a Taoist reading of 'The Old Man and the Sea.'." *The Hemingway Review*, vol. 17, no. 2, 1998, p. 88+. *Literature Resource Center*, go.galegroup.com/ps/i.do?p=GLS&sw=w&u=fjp_jvpl&v=2.1&it=r&id=GALE%7CA20653061&asid=2c4150371338e8fa22c75ff7829bb289. Accessed date.

97. Wagner, Linda W. "The Poem of Santiago and Manolin." *Contemporary Literary Criticism*, edited by Carolyn Riley and Phyllis Carmel Mendelson, vol. 6, Gale, 1976. *Contemporary Literary Criticism Online*, go.galegroup.com/ps/i.do?p=GLS&sw=w&u=fjp_jvpl&v=2.1&it=r&id=GALE%7CJLLODH818397084&asid=8b6cfef7ab34e26bf47dbd8f3bf7cd42. Accessed date. Originally published in *Modern Fiction Studies*, Winter 1973, pp. 517-529.

98. Walcott, Derek. "Hemingway Now." *Twentieth-Century Literary Criticism*, edited by Thomas J. Schoenberg and Lawrence J. Trudeau, vol. 162, Gale, 2005. *Literature Resource Center*, go.galegroup.com/ps/i.do?p=GLS&sw=w&u=fjp_jvpl&v=2.1&it=r&id=GALE%7CH1420064857&asid=9fe70def4ed2b41dfcedf9ea4d84e1d9. Accessed date. Originally published in *North Dakota Quarterly*, vol. 68, no. 2-3, Spring-Summer 2001, pp. 6-13.

99. Waldron, Edward E. "*The Pearl* and *The Old Man and the Sea*: A Comparative Analysis." *Children's Literature Review*, edited by Lawrence J. Trudeau, vol. 194, Gale, 2015. *Literature Resource Center*, go.galegroup.com/ps/i.do?p=GLS&sw=w&u=fjp_jvpl&v=2.1&it=r&id=GALE%7CH1420118518&asid=f37fd132101918917cf5e9654ef0b367. Accessed date.

Originally published in *Steinbeck Quarterly*, vol. 13, no. 3-4, 1980, pp. 98-106.

100. Walz, Lawrence A. "'The Snows of Kilimanjaro': A New Reading." *Short Story Criticism*, edited by Lawrence J. Trudeau, vol. 212, Gale, 2015. *Literature Resource Center*, go.galegroup.com/ps/i.do?p=GLS&sw=w&u=fjp_jvpl&v=2.1&it=r&id=GALE%7CH1420119608&asid=42c5820877f1563cdeb7f2ab3b86dec3. Accessed date. Originally published in *Fitzgerald/Hemingway Annual 1971*, edited by Matthew J. Bruccoli and C. E. Frazer Clark, Jr., NCR/Microcard, 1971, pp. 239-245.

101. Weeks, Robert P. "Fakery in the Old Man and the Sea." *Short Story Criticism*, edited by Anna Sheets-Nesbitt, vol. 36, Gale, 2000. *Short Story Criticism Online*, go.galegroup.com/ps/i.do?p=GLS&sw=w&u=fjp_jvpl&v=2.1&it=r&id=GALE%7CZZIWZT983120011&asid=ad22b0c93df9ad3cbafceea98e2ac548. Accessed date. Originally published in *College English*, vol. 24, no. 3, Dec. 1962, pp. 188-192.

102. West, Ray B, and Ray B. West. "Jr. the Sham Battle over Ernest Hemingway." *Twentieth-Century Literary Criticism*, edited by Janet Witalec, vol. 119, Gale, 2002. *20th Century Literature Criticism Online*, go.galegroup.com/ps/i.do?p=GLS&sw=w&u=fjp_jvpl&v=2.1&it=r&id=GALE%7CBULESC180059228&asid=55a4738a9500f8e2883800acd6c21035. Accessed date. Originally published in *Western Review*, vol. 17, no. 3, Spring 1953, pp. 234-240.

103. Wilson, G. R. "Incarnation and Redemption in the Old Man and the Sea." *Short Story Criticism*, edited by Anna Sheets-Nesbitt, vol. 36, Gale, 2000. *Short Story Criticism Online*, go.galegroup.com/ps/i.do?p=GLS&sw=w&u=fjp_jvpl&v=2.1&it=r&id=GALE%7CSKBSXI685093009&asid=3a5103d8d379f6e34121c9a651f4a675. Accessed date. Originally published in *Studies in Short Fiction*, vol. 14, no. 4, Fall 1977, pp. 369-373.

104. Wittkowski, Wolfgang. "Crucified in the Ring: Hemingway's The Old Man and the Sea." *Short Story Criticism*, edited by Anna Sheets-Nesbitt, vol. 36, Gale, 2000. *Short Story Criticism Online*, go.galegroup.com/ps/i.do?p=GLS&sw=w&u=fjp_jvpl&v=2.1&it=r&id=GALE%7CWFXCAU516873483&asid=4e46160599ed763c350ac6b864eb96ff. Accessed date. Originally published in *The Hemingway Review*, vol. 3, no. 1, Fall 1983, pp. 2-17.

105. Young, Philip. "The Old Man and the Sea: Vision/Revision." *Short Story Criticism*, edited by Anna Sheets-Nesbitt, vol. 36, Gale, 2000. *Short Story Criticism Online*, go.galegroup.com/ps/i.do?p=GLS&sw=w&u=fjp_jvpl&v=2.1&it=r&id=GALE%7CXRWCLB433090547&asid=2ba6377ca79a0eb56710749377b97927. Accessed date. Originally published in *Twentieth-Century Interpretations of The Old Man and the Sea*, Prentice-Hall, Inc., 1968, pp. 18-26.

106. Zeitler, Michael. "Mr. Joe Louis, help me': Sports as Narrative and Community in Ernest J. Gaines's 'A Lesson Before Dying." *Studies in the Literary Imagination*, vol. 49, no. 1, 2016, p.

129+. *Literature Resource Center*, go.galegroup.com/ps/i.do?p=GLS&sw=w&u=fjp_jvpl&v=2.1&it=r&id=GALE%7CA497909577&asid=9c2efecc878f53e5e36d3205dc71cf5c. Accessed date.

Printed in Great Britain
by Amazon